Doctor Nowhere

by Paul S

Illustrated by Bill Ledger

OXFORD
UNIVERSITY PRESS

In this story ...

Ben
(Sprint)

Ben is super fast! He can run faster than a racing car. Once, he ran five times round the school grounds in under ten seconds.

Jin
(Swoop)

Pip
(Boost)

Mr Trainer
(teacher)

Slink
(Combat Cat)

Holohoop

Holohoop is a fast-paced game that tests superheroes' powers and teamwork skills.

hologram hoop

Teams
There are two teams (Team Power and Team Force), each with three players.

Aim
To throw the silver ball through the hologram hoop without touching the hoop. If the ball goes through, there is a loud beep and a point is scored. The team with the most points at the end of the game wins.

Rules
1. The referee starts play by throwing the silver ball into the air and blowing the whistle.
2. Players must spin into their super suits before they can go after the ball.
3. Players may use their superpowers.
4. Players must not touch or bump into each other.

Team Power

Team Force

silver ball

Chapter 1:
The first half

Mr Trainer blew his whistle and threw the silver ball high into the air. The match had begun.

Ben spun into his super suit and became Sprint. He dashed forward ready to catch the ball when it came down. The ball glinted in the sun, far above the heads of the six superheroes.

Holohoop was Sprint's favourite game. Mr Trainer had invented it so his pupils could practise their superpowers. Today, Sprint was in Team Force with Switch and Swoop. To be a good holohoop player, you had to be skilful, fit, and fast. Sprint was fast. *Very* fast.

As the ball came down, Flex stretched to reach it, but Swoop flew in and caught it.

"Swoop!" shouted Sprint, darting across the pitch. "Pass it to me."

Swoop threw the ball. Sprint raced to catch it, but it slipped through his fingers and bounced on the ground. Boost, who was on the other team, grabbed the ball and threw it at the hoop with all her super-strength.

BEEP!

"One-nil," Sprint groaned.

Team Force 0
Team Power 1

Switch turned into an eagle, swooped down, and scored.

Team Force 1
Team Power 1

Invisiboy seized the ball, dodged around Sprint, and scored.

Team Force 1
Team Power 2

Swoop caught the ball, threw it, and scored.

Team Force 2
Team Power 2

Flex snatched the ball just before Sprint could, and scored.

Team Force 2
Team Power 3

Sprint grabbed the ball, ran … and tripped.

Mr Trainer blew his whistle. It was half time. Sprint's team was losing.

Team Force 2
Team Power 3

Boost and Invisiboy flopped down on the grass. Flex dropped down next to them.

Mr Trainer handed out cups of V.V. juice – the vegetable and vitamin blend that boosted the players' energy. Sprint didn't want any.

"No, thanks," he said quietly, shaking his head.

Sprint felt awful. Everyone had scored except for him. He picked up the silver ball and headed back across the pitch to practise on his own. He ran fast, skidded round and threw the ball ... but missed the hoop. He threw again and missed.

"Why can't I throw straight today?" he muttered to himself.

Chapter 2:
The mysterious object

Sprint kept practising. He only stopped because he was getting wheezy. He used his inhaler, sat down on the grass and looked up at the sky. Just then, he saw something strange high above.

Sprint frowned. It was too big to be a bird, too small to be a plane. As it came closer, he saw that it was a parachute. A parachute with a flat, eight-sided shape hanging below it. It was coming down towards the pitch, heading straight for Sprint's friends.

Suddenly, there was a bright flash and a loud *FLICK-FLACK*. The shape underneath the parachute opened up. It had eight sides, which gleamed in the sun, but no top or bottom.

Sprint jumped to his feet. "Watch out!" he shouted to the others, but it was already too late.

The mysterious object landed on the grass, and Mr Trainer and the five superheroes were trapped inside it.

Sprint dashed across the pitch to get a closer look, just as the parachute detached and drifted away. The walls of the object were at least three metres high and made of mirrors. All Sprint could see was his own reflection.

"Hello? Can you hear me?" he shouted to the others.

"Yes," came Mr Trainer's voice from inside, "but we can't see you."

"All we can see are mirrors," said Swoop.

"We can't get out," Boost added.

"Swoop!" Sprint called. "Why don't you just fly out?"

"I can't," Swoop replied. "There's some kind of invisible barrier, like a force field, above our heads. I can't break through it."

"Leave this to me," said Mr Trainer. "I can walk through walls, so I'm sure I can walk through a mirror!" Mr Trainer stepped forward into the mirror ...

... Sprint waited for him to appear. "Mr Trainer?" he called out after a few moments.

"Hasn't he appeared?" Boost shouted. "He's not in here with us!"

"No," Sprint called back in alarm.

"Where's he gone?" Swoop yelled.

"*I'll* tell you where he's gone," came a voice from high above.

Sprint looked up to see a small, red-haired man with a jetpack on his back, hovering in the air above.

Chapter 3:
The Octagone

"Mr Trainer has gone into the mirror," said the red-haired man. "I, Doctor Nowhere, sent him there." He laughed. "Now it's time for you lot to follow him." His laughter got louder as he pressed a button on the remote control in his hand. "You're going *nowhere*!"

Doctor Nowhere

Catchphrase:
You're going *nowhere*!
Hobbies: visiting funfairs and the circus.
Likes: rollercoasters, teddy bears – his favourite is a teddy called Mr Snuggles.
Dislikes: being tickled.
Beware! This villain makes gadgets based on funfairs he's been to. His favourite part of any fair is the hall of mirrors …

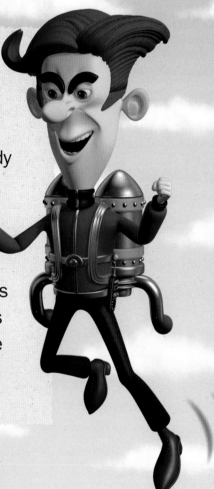

The eight-sided object lifted off the ground by a couple of centimetres. It started to turn in a clockwise direction, slowly at first, but rapidly gathering speed.

"There's a force field below our feet now!" shouted Boost, from inside the object.

"I feel sick," groaned Swoop.

Sprint looked up at Doctor Nowhere, who was still hovering in the air out of reach.

"Why are you doing this?" he demanded.

"I'll tell you why," said Doctor Nowhere, his face twisted with rage. "Many years ago, I wanted to be a hero, but your awful academy turned me away."

Yes, and with good reason.

"Why?" asked Sprint.

"The Head said I *misused* my powers," Doctor Nowhere said with a sneer. "Apparently I'm not allowed to make people I don't like disappear. Well, I'm here to tell you that I can and I will ... with my Octagone – Octa*GONE*, get it?" He laughed. "Say goodbye to your friends!"

By now, the eight-sided object was spinning faster than ever, the mirrors flashing past in a blur. Sprint could hear shouts from inside. He heard Boost's voice: "We're being sucked into the mirrors!"

Sprint gulped. None of his friends appeared on the outside of the Octagone.

Then there was silence.

"Hello?" Sprint called out.

There was no response. He gasped. All his friends had vanished.

"Job done!" said Doctor Nowhere with a smirk. He pressed a button on his remote control, and the Octagone stopped turning.

Sprint frowned. "No one's going to make my friends disappear and get away with it," he said grimly.

"Meow!" said Slink, spinning into Combat Cat.

Chapter 4:
Sprint to the rescue

Sprint raced back across the pitch and grabbed the silver holohoop ball he'd been practising with earlier. He took aim at Doctor Nowhere. This time, he couldn't miss – his friends were relying on him. He took a deep breath and hurled the ball at Doctor Nowhere's jetpack. It was a perfect shot. There was a loud *CRACK* as the ball hit its target.

The jetpack fizzed and smoked, and Doctor Nowhere whizzed around through the air like a balloon that had been blown up and let go. Finally, he flew through the hologram hoop, plunged down and hit the grass. Doctor Nowhere rolled over, looking dazed and confused.

"How can I get my friends back?" said Sprint, striding over to him.

"You can't," Doctor Nowhere said gleefully, scrambling to his feet. "The remote was crushed when I fell."

To his disappointment, Sprint saw the shattered remains of the remote control, where Doctor Nowhere had been lying.

"There must be another way," Sprint said, picking it up.

"Maybe, but I'm not telling," said the villain sulkily.

"Combat Cat," Sprint called out, "do your worst."

Combat Cat didn't need telling twice. He darted forward and began tickling Doctor Nowhere on his tummy and under his arms.

"*Hahaha*. No! No!" Doctor Nowhere spluttered. "Stop … *hahaha* … it!"

"Tell me!" demanded Sprint.

"OK, OK," said Doctor Nowhere, his eyes watering. "To get your friends back, you have to … *hahaha* … spin the Octagone … *hahaha* … back the other way … *hahaha!*"

"That's enough," Sprint told Combat Cat.

Combat Cat dusted his paws and stepped back.

"Keep an eye on him, Combat Cat," Sprint said. "I'm going to try it."

Sprint darted across to the Octagone and started running around it in an anticlockwise direction, pushing the mirrored sides as he ran. It started to turn like a giant roundabout, powered by his legs.

Sprint ran faster, then faster still, until he was racing at super speed.

"Faster!" he muttered, urging himself on. "Faster!"

All of a sudden, Swoop popped out of a mirror and rolled across the grass. The next moment, Boost appeared beside him. Then, on the other side of the spinning Octagone, Flex. Then Switch and Invisiboy.

Sprint kept on running. His legs were a blur.

The last person to land on the grass was
Mr Trainer. He climbed to his feet and did a quick
count of the superheroes.

"We're all back," he announced.

Sprint slowed down, and then stopped running
altogether. Beside him, the Octagone stopped spinning.

Just then, Doctor Nowhere darted across to the Octagone. He reached into his pocket and pulled out a spare remote control. He pressed a button. One of the mirrored panels opened, and he stepped inside.

The Octagone rose high up into the air. Then, with a bright flash and a loud *FLICK-FLACK*, the whole lot disappeared.

"He's gone!" Sprint said, disappointed.

"Don't worry, Sprint," said Mr Trainer, beaming. "You saved us all. Well done!"

Everyone gathered round Sprint. They whooped and cheered.

"Sprint! Sprint! Sprint!" they shouted.

"I couldn't have done it without Combat Cat," Sprint replied.

Mr Trainer laughed and blew his whistle. "Now everyone is back," he said, "it's time for the second half of the holohoop game." He smiled and turned to Sprint. "Although I think we already have our player of the match!"